play infinity

by sondra faye

Printed in the United States of America

First Printing in paperback, 1984 Published by Winston-Derek Publishers

Nashville, Tennessee 37205

Second printing 2015

Library of Congress Catalog Card No: 83-62908

ISBN-10:0692517944
ISBN-13:978-0-692-51794-9
eBook ISBN-10:0692518134
eBook ISBN-13:978-0-692-51813-7

courage to barbara

TABLE OF CONTENTS

play infinity one

✵

your soul can pick anywhere in the universe. and
still you pick here.   why?

play infinity two

A city with no buildings.
A sky with no ceiling
a jungle with no animals
a human without thought
a dimension without hate
life without death
there's no such thing as death.
nothing has a name.
Everything you believe
is everything You believe.
I believe

play infinity three

Time is organization. Institutions
believe in organization. Mankind is
very organized. Men and Women
eat money. Money eats love.
Numbers have meaning on earth.
Murder was invented on earth. People
That commit murder do not want to be
murdered by people that commit murder.
Or vice-versa.
Time is Mentally Evil. Evil
spelt backwards is live, but you
can't spell life backwards and end up with a
word that makes sense.
nothing makes sense to me. Does
nothing make sense to you? If you find
that it does, call me, my phone number is
listed in the universe.

play infinity four

people tell me not to do things.
people tell me not to pick my nose
but they still do it
people tell me not to kill
but they still do it
people tell me not to waste time
but they still do it
people tell me not to cry
but they still do it
people tell me not to hate
but they still do it
people tell me not to leave
but they still do it

I wonder if people will ever tell me not
to listen to people that tell me not
to do things.

play infinity five

I tell people to do things.

play infinity six

Your friends are always trying to get in touch with
  you.
keep your mind open.
Closed minds have narrow hallways. locked doors.
  no keys.
no secrets worth telling. streets with graveyard
  pavement.
for sidewalks that bristleless brush holding painters
  walk
on. empty pocketed with cards that were never given
  numbers.
once inside a closed mind, a painter stood on a
  sidewalk peering
through a 1 ½ meter thick glass at a 2 x 5
  millimeter
sign. the painter didn't know how to read. the
  mind remained
closed.

play infinity seven

an apartment dweller in a metropolis
didn't look out the smudged window
to see the moving television antenna
staring at her. she looked instead at
the carved ivory heart's shadow on
the freshly painted black windowsill.
next to the crumpled and torn black
supple leathered gloves holding onto
each other. then she looked at a closed
book of women's poets. published in 1980. she
didn't know the earliest known writer in the
world. Endeduanna was a sumerian moon
priestess. 2300 B.C. that was a long time ago.
yesterday was a long time ago. tomorrow is
pretty close. she wished it was closer. not
to the point of suicide.

play infinity eight

she knew everything. but everything didn't always
want to talk to her, so everything introduced
her to forget so she could spend some
time with remembering. a close associate
to forget. everything was always at the
apartment dweller's disposal. everything was
always with the apartment dweller.
she went to forget sometimes, and whenever
she left forget, she would always meet
remember. everything was always there.
and she knew everything. and she loved
everything. except forget. she didn't
want to meet forget when she was no longer
an apartment dweller. everything said she
would meet remember. but sometimes forget was
a very good friend to have.

play infinity nine

while on planet earth try very hard to make your
    soul smile.
even if i am dead, i'll smile back. i plan on crying a
    lot of
tears. rain makes things grow. clouds won't hold in
    the rain
too long. they burst and start lightening and
    thundering.
i used to not cry.
sincerely.
i thought it was a foolish effeminate trait.
then i saw a man cry. i changed my
mind. if men can cry, so can women.
i used to do a lot of things, i don't anymore.
i found them ludicrous me traits. one trait i am
holding on to is "i changed my mind." when ever i
    change
my mind
I feel part of the universe.
luckily for me, there's more than one universe.

play infinity ten

before i tell you who i am,
if i don't make love soon, i think i'm going
to be very horney. i don't mind being very horney,
just as long as i know i won't
be very horney for long. making love is a
creative process. celibacy is one form of
that creative process. celibacy is one form of
that creative process. i think celibates
masturbate a lot. i prefer making love
with another human being, but sometimes
the situation calls for celibacy.
oh, i'm happy to tell you that the
human being i make love with is
coming in to new york town tomorrow.
i am new york town.

play infinity eleven

mystic celibates suffocate in warped ritualistic
   atmosphere.
heavenly denunciations unfold lies untold.
   unthinking non-
believers masticate garbled clichés in alacritous
   movement.
listen. to their difficult gut spilling denunciations.
   it's
hard to listen to stories of fictional lives you do not
   lead.
to people committed not to bleed in public places.
yes, i think i'm going to stay home tonight. i'm
   energetically
self-contained.

play infinity twelve

i went to a party last year. it was a social gathering.
i wasn't overtly sociable. i was friendly. i'm always
friendly. i'm always silent. I, am always alone.
   except
sometimes. You made me feel like i was on the
   same trip
with another human being. I loved You very much
   for that.
I hope you know.

play infinity thirteen

✸

i'm scared. maybe human beings aren't supposed
    to be
scared. but i am anyway. i'm going to take my
life into my own hands. it always worked out
    before.
it will again.

play infinity fourteen

take a cube. throw it in the air. leave
it there. in suspension. watch it explode
into tiny little particles. a cube. a cube.
a cube. a cube. a cube. a cube. a cube.
take all those cubes in your hands then
throw them in the air and leave them
there. in suspension. watch them all
explode into particles. a cube. a cube.
a cube. back to one cube. silly you, how
can you go back? even if you play
casablanca backwards, you're playing
humphrey bogart backwards now. so why go back
to one cube? take a cube. a cube. a cube.
a cube. a cube. a cube. a cube. if at first
you get one cube, watch it shatter into many
cubes. then watch many cubes in suspension
shatter into a circle. take a circle.
throw it in the air. leave it there. in
suspension. watch it explode. expand into
a sphere. leave it there. take
you. throw yourself into the air. leave
you there. in suspension. watch you
explode into tiny particles. a you. a you.

a you. a you. quadrophenia. schizophrenia?
growth of creativity. picasso still
explodes. and you and you and you and
you still explodes.

play infinity fifteen

✵

if you are reading this
the following question applies to you:
who do you love?
no names, please.

play infinity sixteen

the twentieth century fallacy is cars. henry ford
helped drive people. cars began making people
at the onset of the industrial revolution. the
bourgeois cars would drive people to local
supermarkets and leave their people in the
parking lots so they could buy food. sometimes
people that were left in the parking lots would
get dented or receive fender benders by other
people driven by bourgeois cars. cars knew
people would eventually rust, so cars especially
traveling sales cars would buy new people every
two years, or so with the help of henry ford
type favorites. people one day became obsolete.
most cars never thought they could invent a better
means of transportation than people. but look
how wrong cars can be.

play infinity seventeen

lost innocence. pressurized rose petals smash in
  center
place. once in a rose garden. once in boston. chilly
  lion
cut subtle neck. lamb's marbles rolled down one
  way street.
little berkeley boys shoot eyes into guitars and
  saxophones.
they play jazz. lamb played naïve. lamb lost. lamb
  became
lion. lion locks with black and white marbleized
  eyes. lion
wins. lions always do. and lambs successfully get
  slaughtered
entering rose gardens. there's no rose gardens in
  nyc. only
glass coffers holding freshly frozen rose petals.

play infinity eighteen

i lost. didn't mean to. didn't want to. it happened.

i fought. didn't mean to. didn't want to. it
  happened.

i live. didn't mean to. didn't want to. it happened.

play infinity nineteen

i have a part of you. do you have a part
of me? i want to have another part
of you. do you want to have another
part of me? i desire everything
you willingly can share with me.
do you desire everything i willingly
can share with you? i need you
in my life, in my mind, in my heart, in
my body, in my world. i need you for
real. do you need me like i need you?
am i real to you? do you dream about
me? i dream about you. i thought for
a while it would stop. it did. it
started again. that's why i need you.
if i really stopped needing
you. if i really stopped dreaming about
you. think about this, why would it
have started again. it is you. and it is
you i need.

play infinity twenty

fiction upon fiction. results numerous sordid
   stories.
mind mutilations with video distortions as contrast.
exhibit: persons unknown. more foreign bodies
   moving
towards the carnivorous. jumping inside. jumping
   out.
carnivorous, in past history fictions, can not remain
   in
control of foreign bodies. foreign bodies contain
friction. friction contains moving parts. this is not
geometric friction. love. energy. or you me. positive
identification surfaces. existence.

play infinity twenty-one

when i read the words that aren't written, i think
  i'm
a genius. when i read the words that are written, i
  think
i'm reading. when i think i'm a genius, i think i can
  solve
the world's problems. when i think i can solve the
  world's
problems, i know i am dreaming.

play infinity twenty-two

secret ceremonious glazed eyed cats. double
  identity. public
unaware. brown tufted black cats don't care.
  separate secluded
world intrinsically isomorphic. not sphynx nor man
  nor in
average suburbanite plan. queen's habitation.
  effectual
hesitating young grimalkins. untouched triangles.
  at least
one remained virginal. no wedding bed reds. only
  gold rings
chastising mouths giving head. plastic fingers
  without
procreating powers. camouflage children in
  photographed
box of paint. slapped on canvas. feeding on edible
  air breasts.
maturing into conversational masterpieces.
  transcending
nature's way towards effeminate plato effusion.

play infinity twenty-three

platinum covered silhouette. timorous girl
  virginette.
hold me tomorrow. apex knowingly cherished. by
  me,
solamente. shall we enter the passionate inferno?
is it detrimental to throw away plato's idealistic
  love?
touch me yesterday. incandescent tattered heart. i
  saw
tremble. hold me angel. no touch unfathomable.

play infinity twenty-four

mind explosion. heart expansion. intransigent
  acceptance.
of relationship with you. territorial intrusion upon
lifetime solutions made in moments.

play infinity twenty-five

other's think we lie. but you and i understand what
  we're
going through together. love is ill-conceived by
  those who
ascertain man-woman relationship must
  continually plead guilty
of insanity. certainly there are times i fantasize of
  stepping
behind the thin line of sensual friendship. putting
  on the
mask of lover. consummation. i see your empty
  moon behind
linear mountains. boston's not that far away from
  new york
city. you're always with me in my masked role of
  insanity
telling true confessions to the real world. but when
  i take
off the mask, i have nothing to confess. as far as
  my masks
go, whenever you see them, you act blind. you do
  play fair.

i guess i shouldn't get mad when you reveal my self
    to us.
don't laugh when i say i'm tough inside, must the
    other's
find out that i'm terribly shy, romantically
    susceptible,
and guilty of holding on to obscenely illustrated
    notecards
you send me from boston?

play infinity twenty-six

You had a beasty good idea. you invented waste
   disposals.
multicolored and achromatic. multitudes crowding
   in subway
grey hallways needed the idea. you refused to show
   anyone
the good idea. apathy insisted this was the correct
   thing
to do in your situation. multitudes began
   accumulating trash.
the acquisition of trash was a requirement for the
   multi.
reversion swept you into the trash. you forgot a
   good idea.
i'm here to remind you, that you had a beasty.

play infinity twenty-seven

listening solutions. absurd romantic tunes.
   distraughtful
evening resolution. embarked encounters
   misconstrued. sinful
mate, younker telephone rings. pink up no answer.
   put down
receiver no question. don't think twice. neglectful
   word
encounter. non-thinking i love yous. juvenile
   misconceptions.
don't say i love you if you don't know what it
   means.
break an egg, then bring it to me. useless white
   shells
throw away. yolk and egg white craving. let us
   ignite ardent
yellow. slowly? or with passion. definitely the latter.

play infinity twenty-eight

you ask me what you should do in life. immediately
   i answer,
don't ask me what you should do in life. do i have
   to tell you
everything? can't you go out into the world on your
   own and
make your own messes instead of cleaning up
   messes
someone else tells you to make? you're so damn
   afraid of
the real world. i guess
that is your world.

play infinity twenty-nine

oh go ahead, go turn on the cable t.v., and
  whatever you do,
don't ask me why you're not meeting anybody.

play infinity thirty

It is the act, not the watching of. It is the
   undetermined
future, not the finished past. It is the player, not
   the play.
it is the kill, not the dead meat. It is the baking of
   bread, not
the defecation of food. It is the lit cigarette, not the
   ashes.
laying wasted in an ashtray. It is the champagne on
   ice, not
the unopened bottle waiting to be bought in the
   liquor store.
It is the brush in hand with linseed oil on boar's
   hair, not
the dry masterpiece forsaken in a mausoleum. It is
page fifty-
two of the manuscript, not the three hundred page
   novel underneath
the dictionary on the student's desk. It is the word
   yet to be
said, not the remembrance of dissipated
   conversation. It is
the fingers hitting flats and sharps, not the stereo

playing

harmony. It is the changes, not adherence to an
    arrangement.

It is the search, not the tone after the exclamation
    of discovery.

It is the unthought of, not the known.

play infinity thirty-one

concentric conversations permeate diluting yellow
  patterns
rearrange forming tension sculptures. jagged
  edges puzzle
apart. torn together. rip. rip. rip. the pages from
  the book and
there will be no story for anyone other than
  yourself.
unequivocal masterpieces left untold. only you
  hold the end
in sight. pernicious justifications say they of your
  genius.
keep courage, stay unrelenting. sacrifice is
  superficial.
tradition is dead. life surpasses it. succumb to no
  one
else's morals. and make yours momentary.
  steadfastness is
pretentious and you'll only ridicule your future.
serious
comical tragic elations transmigrate.

play infinity thirty-two

sophisticated droplet of champagne slips out of
  crackle cut
goblet. whipping through space. frozen on
  polished glass
temptation. scum nonexistant. impurities
  stagnated. performance
thus begins.

play infinity thirty-three

i think we started something. maybe the game is
   chess. rather
idealistic. only two players. inevitable movements.
   vehement
kings never touch in vain. the dynamism of sport
   continues
after fatal graze. mechanical molten statues lucidly
   slip
through the crack. and begin the game off the
   board. otherwise
remain space descendants moving square to
   square. never winning
never losing. never getting anywhere. we're not
   kings. there's
no right or wrong or win or lose in this reckless
   game we
play. your move.

play infinity thirty-four

your smile in the dark made my smile in the dark
  happen. cause
and effect. brown cotton shadows covered us. itchy
  woolen
blankets too. plum wine, newport legere cigarillos.
  minus
champagne, silky negligee and chocolate covered
  roses. minus
dainties unlike pizza flavored ambrosia. still i felt
  venus
and mars watching over. cupid caught you off
  guard when you
tasted tristan's rootbeer, as for me, i had a taste of
iseult's capuccino. made mostly of scalded milky
  cream.
please don't tell me if you think what i next will say
  is
true. was it just a dream? or did cupid accurately
  shoot his
arrow through not one but two virgin lovers
  holding only
one another.

our love is laughter. we're being taught happiness.
    when the
lesson's over
-all too soon -together.
knowledge will tell us what comes after.

play infinity thirty-five

✵

planetary associations, ambitious you, ambitious
  me, sexual
persuasion tenaciously duplistic. in a millisecond
  thoughts
transcend into my compartment. where did you
  find my key?
unsuccessful brick doors unmortared by your spy
  tendencies.
how about me? can i have private affairs, if you're a
  private
eye? please send advice, or clue, must you know my
  other
mister who? is this game candid? unbiased
  opinions accept
outright. knowledge attained, possibly jealousy
  gained. under
guidance telescopes watch changeable stars. velvet
  stars
associate. brushed one way, brushed another duo
  color

retrospection secondary. unnecessary for creation.

  silent

future stars stripped velvet. velvet goes either, or.

stars go.

play infinity thirty-six

only touch me your way. autumn fingers change
   my colors.
let's play.

play infinity thirty-seven

i saw a move at loews cinema house near broadway
   with a
friend. i don't know why, but when he put his arm
   around me,
i thought a shadow screamed don't let him! and
   when i was in
the subway station on the way there, i thought any
   moment i
would run into you. and when he and i were
   walking out of the
cinema, i thought surely i would bump into you.
   and when he
and i were walking down the street, and i was
   holding his
sweaty palm in my tensely dry hand, i thought,
   hell i know
i'm indubitably going to crash into you on the
   street, and
when he entered my apartment, i practically threw
rimbaud's a season in hell and the illuminations at him as my
   white
push button telephone rang. i thought, this is it, it
   would

be unreasonable to think anyone else but you
  would call. and
when i pushed him out the door twenty minutes
  later after i
had gotten off from the phone conversation with
  my friend
from israel, i thought how am i going to tell that
  friend
that i want to continue having a platonic affair. and
  all the
times when i thought i was going to run into you i
  kept on
wondering why i wanted to tell you i'm beginning
  to feel like
pinnochio.

play infinity thirty-eight

it was a dream we had together. it was a thought we
  thought of
first. it was illusion to exist. and yet we touch and
  think
and feel. and yet we know that we are real. sorrow
  brings
joy with pain of knowing you. i show you
  everything. you want
more. my soul is mine. ask not for it, you'll receive
  more.
i don't give my self away like i used to. i give
  wisdom.
something no lover ever bargained for. ex-fuckers
  tried to
buy me. wrap me in leather, jewels and silk. that's
  why
they're ex-fuckers. i read the ending first when i
  wrote their
stories. you're not fiction to me. swallow that.
  you're not
even a fuck. yet. i will never write your story, you're
  not

singular to me. we'll never know the end to our
  story, so i'll
leave traces of our dream for another ambitious
  writer's
novelistic scheme. i can't write this play anyway. i'm
  one of
the main characters.

play infinity thirty-nine

i feel your pain in the dark. when i breathe i feel
   your
heart. image sensation enters my body. i gasp. your
   image
rips right through me.
i can't even cry.
i can't even sleep.
i know you travel to me in the night. and my astral
   body
makes love with your astral body in another
   dimension. if
you think i don't know this is happening, think
   again.
cause every time you feel me is every time i feel
   you.

play infinity forty

fearful thoughts contain me sometimes. life
   without you seems
unimaginable. and yet it's a possibility. don't tell me
   not to
think about it. i'd rather face the reality of losing
   you now,
than naively anticipating eternity's false pretense
   and acting
like you don't mean anything to me while i still
   have you in
my now.

play infinity forty-one

once you're against something you have created a
   negative
energy. negative energies drift into space.
   continual
uncontrolled concepts. relative accidental reactions.
intangible conundrums. compulsory optimistic
   suppression.
paranoid? careful next opportunity.

play infinity forty-two

✴

love is always moving towards you

play infinity forty-three

man once thought there was no such thing as
  woman. man once
thought there was no such thing as man. man once
  thought
there was no such thing as make-believe. man lied.

play infinity forty-four

enter the eternal marathon unknown to those who
do not question.

play infinity forty-five

see. want. desire. the object. capability of
   deception. naïve
substitution policy. daring duo amoeba.
biological counterfeit
accepted without guaranteed return.
   materialistics
procreate inconspicuous servile amoeba. duo
   amoeba releases
into singular formation undaunted. again the
   object. erase
desire—want—see—

play infinity forty-six

selfish hours spent characterizing words.
  completion, happiness.
yesterday's unsought pleasures today recognized
  influential
pressures. worried moments futile. action utilized.
  unlimiting
life sustaining elements turn fortunes price into
  latent fame.
no one knows except you. decision. prefabricated
  future
suspensions. the meditative quest.

play infinity forty-seven

classifications determine carnivorous. classifications
are real. classifications determining carnivorous are
illusory. uncontrolled determine classifications.
recognizable media stimulants disregard natural
   elements.
mass dissolves into drones. drones exalt imbecilic
classifications. tendencies to abbreviate multiply.
forthcoming computers increase divisionism. elitist
set aside humanitarian principles. developmental
elitism is anarchical towards society. society blurps
vulnerability. ignorance breeds fear. elitist control
drones.

play infinity forty-eight

the computer said you're wasting your life. the
    computer said
you're outdated. the computer said it was more
    intelligent than
you. the computer said at least it didn't have to
    worry about
gaining weight, wrinkles or overdue bills. the
    computer said
you're helplessly terminal. the computer smiled
    computers
live forever. the computer programmer punched
    the data
processing button and typed: computers suck.
    computers suck.
computers suck. computers suck. computers suck.
    computers suck.
... the computer programmer smiled. then after a
    thousand
computer suck's later, turned the computer off.

play infinity forty-nine

too sentimental said the english professor to the
    student.
that's what's wrong with poets. so when you read
    poetry that's
fallen into this category, view it as an adult would—
skeptically and never letting yourself feel to the
    enth
degree as the poet did. you will be graded on your
insensitivity said the poet to the english professor.

play infinity fifty

could it be you? no, no, no, no, no, no. you just
   look like someone
that could be you. you're wearing that plastic mask.
   how do
i know? silly, silly. but of course i have one too. only
strangers find it obsequious to put on plastic
   masks. you
never could admit to snapping a stranger's
   portrait. so
what is the matter with portraying a tourist?

play infinity fifty-one

little people never say that they are little people.
  bothersome
big people find contentment in reminding
  little people
that they are indeed little people. however, little
  people
do not accept satisfaction by being reminded that
  they are
little people. in fact, the reason why big people
  always tell
little people they are little, is because they have to
  remind
themselves that they are big.

play infinity fifty-two

thumbed through newspapers. propaganda media
  puppets. you're
never quite sure who to believe, turned on
  television.
peoploids paid for promulgating institutional
  chicanery.
you wonder if they believe what they're telling you.
  soft
spoken radio announcers lisping absurdities while
  you're
sleeping. and you dream. after all, they can't tell
  you how
to do that.

play infinity fifty-three

labyrinthine religious phenomenon. explicating
  messiahs
disavowing predecessors. tormented leaders always
  seem to
be smeared by unjustified accusations. religion is
  big
business nowadays. if they're really preaching love,
  why do
they need money?

play infinity fifty-four

there should be no such thing as money, murder,
   war, jealousy,
hate, starvation, disease, and a few other things.
there should be such a thing as love and peace and
   a
few other things.

play infinity fifty-five

✵

read this carefully, slowly, diligently. this could be
   the
last thing that you'll ever read.

play infinity fifty-six

have no fear child, inside of you is everything you'll ever need to know.

play infinity fifty-seven

and why were you born?

play infinity fifty-eight

❂

you can think up a better excuse than that.

play infinity fifty-nine

when the world began, there was peace. after many
  years, there
evolved a human species with two sexes, male,
female. after
many years of mating, eating sleeping, pissing,
  shitting, there
were wars. after many years of creative killing,
  there were historians to tell about progress. after many years
  of storytelling
there were many absent minded people who
  refused to
listen.
when the world began, there was

play infinity sixty

so you think it is impossible. everyone else agrees.
  they're
laughing through your tears. you shouldn't dream
  such tremendous
dreams. at every rehearsal they tell you stop
  thinking about it.
i hope you never listen to them when they tell you
  not to
dream. i never did. except once. one fatalistic night
  upon
contemplation of suicide. i really thought they had
  me down.
i really thought my dreams were nonexistent as far
  as
attainment. i played limitations. now, i play infinity

play infinity sixty-one

❈

you never know when your dreams are going to
come true